YOU
ARE SO
AWESOME

summersdale

YOU ARE SO AWESOME

Compiled by Peggy Jones

An Hachette UK Company
www.hachette.co.uk

Summersdale Publishers
Part of Octopus Publishing Group Limited
Carmelite House
50 Victoria Embankment
LONDON
EC4Y 0DZ
UK

www.summersdale.com

Printed and bound in China

ISBN: 978-1-83799-353-6

Substantial discounts on bulk quantities of Summersdale books are available to corporations, professional associations and other organizations. For details contact general enquiries: telephone: +44 (0) 1243 771107 or email: enquiries@summersdale.com.

To...

From.......................................

We are who we know ourselves to be, and we are what we love.

Laverne Cox

Those who bring
sunshine into the
lives of others
cannot keep it
from themselves.

J. M. Barrie

Never doubt your inner magic

IF MY MIND CAN CONCEIVE IT, AND MY HEART CAN BELIEVE IT, THEN I CAN ACHIEVE IT.

Muhammad Ali

Be yourself; everyone else is already taken.

Anonymous

I was made exactly the way I was meant to be made.

Megan Rapinoe

KEEP ON
GROWING

You are not a drop in the ocean. You are the entire ocean in a drop.

Rumi

Find out who
you are and love
who you are.

Zendaya

YOU'RE
MEANT TO
BE YOU

It's only your
opinion that
matters in your
life and in your
self-love and
your self-worth.

Billie Eilish

You define
your own life.
Don't let other
people write
your script.

Oprah Winfrey

We must have perseverance and above all confidence in ourselves.

Marie Curie

Never apologize for who you are

I SCORCHED
THE EARTH
WITH MY
TALENT
**AND I LET
MY LIGHT
SHINE.**

André Leon Talley

Accept no one's definition of your life, but define yourself.

Harvey Fierstein

LET THE
VOICE
WITHIN
YOU SING

You can be
everything.
You can be the
infinite amount
of things that
people are.

Kesha

Why should I care what other people think of me? I am who I am. And who I wanna be.

Avril Lavigne

You've always
had the power
my dear, you just
had to learn it
for yourself.

L. Frank Baum

BE BRAVE:
GO FORTH
AND LOVE
YOURSELF

It's OK to change your mind a million times and figure out what works for you. It's OK to take your time.

Amandla Stenberg

When you take care of yourself, you're a better person for others. When you feel good about yourself, you treat others better.

Solange Knowles

Your difference is your power

Don't give up
trying to do
what you really
want to do.

Ella Fitzgerald

AS SOON
AS YOU
TRUST
YOURSELF,
YOU WILL
KNOW HOW
TO LIVE.

Johann Wolfgang von Goethe

You alone are enough. You have nothing to prove to anybody.

Maya Angelou

You are
so strong

I am not afraid of storms, for I am learning how to sail my ship.

Louisa May Alcott

Everyone has inside of him a piece of good news. The good news is that you don't know how great you can be!

Anne Frank

YOUR
DREAMS
WILL GUIDE
THE WAY

Love the
life you live.
Live the life
you love.

Bob Marley

If we could just celebrate all the wonderful complexities of people, the world would be such a better place.

Elliot Page

You are worthy.

Demi Lovato

Be bold,
be wild

You are the one
that possesses
the keys to your
being. You carry
the passport to
your own happiness.

Diane von Fürstenberg

YOU HAVE TO GO THE WAY YOUR BLOOD BEATS.

James Baldwin

IF IT FEELS
RIGHT, IT
IS RIGHT

I know not all that
may be coming,
but be it what
it will, I'll go to
it laughing.

Herman Melville

You are beautiful and you are strong and you are worth it.

Jordin Sparks

Treat yourself like you'd treat your best friend.

Jameela Jamil

A LITTLE SELF-LOVE GOES A LONG WAY

Don't try to
lessen yourself
for the world;
let the world
catch up to you.

Beyoncé

I celebrate myself, and sing myself.

Walt Whitman

Love yourself, always and forever

The challenge is not to be perfect – it is to be whole.

Jane Fonda

You've got to love
yourself first.

Jennifer Lopez

Act as
if what you
do makes a
difference.
It does.

William James

SMILE ON YOUR FACE, SELF-BELIEF IN YOUR HEART

YOU ARE ENOUGH JUST AS YOU ARE.

Meghan, Duchess of Sussex

It takes courage
to grow up and
become who
you really are.

E. E. Cummings

Make
a habit
of loving
yourself

**No one
is useless in
this world
who lightens
the burdens
of another.**

Charles Dickens

Every one of us needs to show how much we care for each other and, in the process, care for ourselves.

Diana, Princess of Wales

**Know your
own happiness.**

Jane Austen

You always had what it takes

**Dwell on
the beauty of
life. Watch the
stars, and see
yourself running
with them.**

Marcus Aurelius

Owning our story and loving ourselves through that process is the bravest thing we'll ever do.

Brené Brown

CHOOSE YOUR OWN HAPPINESS EVERY TIME

Believe you
can and you're
halfway there.

Theodore Roosevelt

LIFE IS A CLIMB, BUT THE VIEW IS GREAT.

Miley Cyrus

Beauty is everywhere. You only have to look to see it.

Bob Ross

FALL IN LOVE WITH YOUR TRUE SELF

If you hear a voice within you say "you cannot paint", then by all means paint, and that voice will be silenced.

Vincent van Gogh

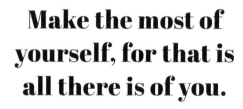

Make the most of yourself, for that is all there is of you.

Ralph Waldo Emerson

You can't
dim my
awesomeness

If I cannot do
great things, I can
do small things
in a great way.

Martin Luther King Jr

**Being happy
never goes
out of style.**

Lilly Pulitzer

Acknowledge the good, because there is always a lot of good.

Kerry Washington

BE TRUE TO YOURSELF AND YOU CAN'T GO WRONG

With confidence,
you have won
even before you
have started.

Cicero

THERE ARE AS MANY KINDS OF LOVE AS THERE ARE HEARTS.

Leo Tolstoy

Just keep going and keep that energy flowing

How you love
yourself is how
you teach others
to love you.

Rupi Kaur

If we all did the things we are capable of doing, we would literally astound ourselves.

Thomas Edison

There is no way to be perfect and no fun in being perfect.

Alicia Keys

No one
else can
be you,
remember
that

It is so important to take time for yourself and find clarity. The most important relationship is the one you have with yourself.

Diane von Fürstenberg

**Never bend
your head.
Always hold it
high. Look the
world straight
in the eye.**

Helen Keller

Grow, glow,
and go for it!

It sounds so simple, but if you just be yourself, you're different than anyone else.

Tony Bennett

Don't waste your
energy trying to
change opinions…
Do your thing,
and don't care
if they like it.

Tina Fey

BE BOLD, BE BRAVE ENOUGH TO BE YOUR TRUE SELF.

Queen Latifah

HONOUR YOUR OWN POWER

I like me.
I like my story
and all the
bumps and
bruises. That's
what makes me
uniquely me.

Michelle Obama

If you see someone without a smile, give 'em yours!

Dolly Parton

You can never have too much time for yourself

Wanting to be someone else is a waste of the person you are.

Kurt Cobain

Embrace your
weirdness.

Cara Delevingne

Beauty is how you feel inside, and it reflects in your eyes. It is not something physical.

Sophia Loren

LET YOUR
MAGIC LEAD
THE WAY

Loving yourself isn't vanity. It's sanity.

André Gide

The greatest thing
in the world is
to know how to
belong to oneself.

Michel de Montaigne

You're
unstoppable

There is
always light.
If only we're
brave enough
to see it. If only
we're brave
enough to be it.

Amanda Gorman

ALWAYS BE YOURSELF AND HAVE FAITH IN YOURSELF.

Bruce Lee

It took me quite a long time to develop a voice, and now that I have it, I am not going to be silent.

Madeleine Albright

When you steer your own ship, you can go anywhere

Don't you ever let a soul in the world tell you that you can't be exactly who you are.

Lady Gaga

The light of
love is always in
us, no matter how
cold the flame.

bell hooks

ACTUALLY, YOU CAN

Love yourself first
and everything else
falls into line.

Lucille Ball

Follow your inner moonlight.

Allen Ginsberg

The only thing that
will make you happy
is being happy
with who you are.

Goldie Hawn

FEEL YOUR
SOUL TAKE
CONTROL

Inspiration comes from within yourself. One has to be positive. When you're positive, good things happen.

Deep Roy

YOU
CHANGE
THE
WORLD
**BY BEING
YOURSELF.**

Yoko Ono

When your
heart speaks,
listen

**All dreams
are within reach.
All you have to do
is keep moving
towards them.**

Viola Davis

Owning who you are and knowing what you want is the only sure path to affirmation.

Ashley Graham

It's better to
be absolutely
ridiculous than
absolutely boring.

Marilyn Monroe

YOU'RE
PRETTY
SPECIAL

What is fundamentally beautiful is compassion; for yourself and for those around you.

Lupita Nyong'o

Happiness is the best makeup.

Drew Barrymore

Today, be no
one but you

All you can
do is be your
best self.

Misty Copeland

IF YOU HAVE THE ABILITY TO LOVE, **LOVE YOURSELF FIRST.**

Charles Bukowski

To shine your brightest light is to be who you truly are.

Roy T. Bennett

Be proud in your power

**Go boldly
and honestly
through the world.
Learn to love the
fact that there
is nobody else
quite like you.**

Daniel Radcliffe

The mere sense of living is joy enough.

Emily Dickinson

YOU WERE
BORN TO
STAND OUT

Just be
yourself,
there is no
one better.

Taylor Swift

Beauty is when you can appreciate yourself. When you love yourself, that's when you're most beautiful.

Zoë Kravitz

Whatever you do, be different.

Anita Roddick

YOU
ALREADY
KNOW WHO
YOU ARE:
BE IT

I don't
like myself.
I'm crazy
about myself.

Mae West

NEVER DULL YOUR SHINE FOR SOMEBODY ELSE.

Tyra Banks

You
deserve
it all

A person learns how to love himself through the simple acts of loving and being loved by someone else.

Haruki Murakami

Once you face your fear, nothing is ever as hard as you think.

Olivia Newton-John

Make the most of yourself by fanning the tiny, inner sparks of possibility into flames of achievement.

Golda Meir

YOU HAVE
PERMISSION
TO BE
YOURSELF

Do the things
that interest you
and do them with
all your heart.

Eleanor Roosevelt

Derive your worth from things that are truly important like real relationships and your relationship with yourself.

Olivia Rodrigo

Shine on,
shine bright

"Who am I to be brilliant, gorgeous, talented, fabulous?" Actually, who are you not to be?

Marianne Williamson

Being yourself
is all it takes.

Selena Gomez

I TO
MYSELF AM
**DEARER
THAN A
FRIEND.**

William Shakespeare

Do it for yourself

Different is good...
When someone
tells you that you
are different,
smile, and hold
your head up
and be proud.

Angelina Jolie

Never allow someone to be your priority while allowing yourself to be their option.

Mark Twain

LOVE
YOURSELF
EXACTLY
AS YOU
ALREADY ARE

Do not bend yourself to make others feel taller.

Rose McGowan

I am my
own experiment.
I am my own
work of art.

Madonna

**Confidence
is the most
beautiful
thing you
can possess.**

Sabrina Carpenter

THIS IS
YOUR STORY

You have to
be able to love
yourself because
that's when things
fall into place.

Vanessa Hudgens

Normal is not
something to aspire
to, it's something
to get away from.

Jodie Foster

DON'T LOSE SIGHT OF YOUR STRENGTH

YOU ARE
YOUR BEST
THING.

Toni Morrison

Just believe in yourself. Even if you don't, pretend that you do and, at some point, you will.

Venus Williams

The one thing that you have that nobody else has is you.

Neil Gaiman

Who wants to be
normal when you
can be unique?

Helena Bonham Carter

The only thing you need to wear well is your confidence.

Priyanka Chopra

YOU ARE SO
AWESOME

Have you enjoyed this book?
If so, find us on Facebook at
Summersdale Publishers,
on Twitter/X at @Summersdale
and on Instagram and TikTok at
@summersdalebooks and get in touch.
We'd love to hear from you!

www.summersdale.com